SCOUT SKITS

A collection of more than 100 favorite campfire skits

Thomas Mercaldo

Printed in the United States.
Eighth Printing.

For ordering information, see page 56.

Aquinas Scout Books
C/O Thomas C. Mercaldo
154 Herbert Street
Milford, CT 06461

Scout Fun Books is not officially affiliated with the Boy Scouts of America, Girl Scouts of America, Scouts Canada or the World Organization of Scouting.

Scout Fun Books can be purchased on a wholesale basis for resale in Camp Stores, Scout Shops and Trading Posts. For details write to us at the above address or contact us by email at BoyScoutBooks@aol.com. For individual orders see page 56.

How to use this book

Listed at the beginning of each skit are the number of participants required and any props which may be needed. Generally, there is a minimum number needed to perform each skit, however, additional participants can usually be added. The dialog between participants is in plain text, while instructions for actors are listed in italics. An index is available at the end of this book which references skits by subject matter. Variations, when they exist, follow each skit.

Preface

During my many years in Scouting, I have had the opportunity to participate in many campfires. The performance of a new skit can be the highlight of a week at summer camp. Scouts like to perform skits, but generally, they have a limited knowledge of possible skits, so the same skits tend to be performed over and over again. Scout Skits is my attempt to re-introduce some popular old skits to younger Scouts. Additionally, Scout Skits catalogs most of the skits that are popular today, and introduces some new skits that I have authored.

I sincerely hope that you enjoy Scout Skits, and that it helps you create outstanding campfires. Special thanks go to those who contributed to this effort. They include Paul Kallmeyer and Joseph Bajek two longtime scouting friends, and Renee Allen who performed the proofreading.

I hope you enjoy reading this book as much as I enjoyed putting it together.

Tom Mercaldo

Share Your Favorite Skit with Us

Know a new skit? We invite you to send us campfire skits that you might like to see included in our next campfire skit book. We will consider any skit that you feel Scouts might enjoy seeing performed at a campfire. Send your submissions to:

Aquinas Scout Fun Books
Attention: Tom Mercaldo
154 Herbert Street
Milford, CT 06461
Or by email to: ScoutBooks@aquinasconsulting.com

We hope you enjoy reading this book as much as we enjoyed putting it together.

Table of Contents

Is it Time Yet?

Participants: 4 to 5.
Props: A wrist watch.

To perform this skit, a group of 4 or 5 Scouts sit on a bench or log with their legs crossed, right leg over left. The Scout at the left end of the log turns to his right and asks the question, "Is it time yet?" The Scout to his right responds, "I don't know," and turns to his right and asks, "Is it time yet?" This is repeated until the question reaches the end Scout who looks at his watch and responds, "Not yet." The first Scout then once again asks the question and the process is repeated a second time. On the third pass the final Scout in the chain replies, "Yep, it's time," and together the Scouts lower their right legs and re-cross their legs with the left leg now on top.

Rough Riders

Participants: 5 to 7.
Props: Sleeping bags.

Two Scouts are laying on sleeping bags, one is in a tent, the other just outside it. A group of bikers come by and say, "Hey, let's beat up on this guy in the sleeping bag." Upset by this incident the Scout in the sleeping bag wakes up his friend in the tent and tells him what happened. The Scout in the tent dismisses the story, explaining that the whole thing must have been a bad dream. The Scout in the tent commands the other to go back to sleep. A few minutes later the bikers come back and again beat on the Scout sleeping outside. After they leave, he arouses his friend who again tells him it was just a dream. However, to make him feel safer they agree to change places. The bikers come back a third time and the skit ends with one of the bikers saying, "This guy's had enough, let's get the guy in the tent this time."

Painter's Canvas

Participants: 3 to 5.
Props: Several drawings or paintings.

This skit takes place at an art show. Several snooty art critics are examining the canvas's that are displayed. They are very critical until they come to one canvas which they believe is "A brilliant work of art," "Sheer genius," "An exquisite beauty," etc. They choose this canvas for a prize and call up the winning artist. The painter exclaims, "Oh my gosh! that got in by mistake. That's the canvas I use to clean my brushes!"

Campfire Beverages

Participants: 4.
Props: A large pot and 3 coffee mugs.

Scout 1: (*Walks up to the pot, dips in his coffee mug and brings it up to his lips for a sip*).
This campfire coffee is terrible.

Scout 2: (*Walks up to the pot, dips in his coffee mug and brings it up to his lips for a sip*).
This campfire tea is terrible.

Scout 3: (*Walks up to the pot, dips in his coffee mug and brings it up to his lips for a sip*).
This campfire hot chocolate is terrible.

Scout 4: (*Walks up to the pot, dips in his hands in and takes out a pair of wet socks, he wrings them out as he says:*).
I thought this would get them clean.

You can follow this skit up with a brief one-liner

Scout 1: This coffee tastes like mud.
Scout 2: That's funny, it was just ground this morning.

Pentholl, Pentholl

Participants: 4.
Props: Pencils.

Scout 2 addresses Scout 1.

Scout 2:   Okay now I want you to sell these pencils.

Scout 1:   Pentholls?

Scout 2:   That's right, pencils.   When you see someone coming, be sure to tell them what you are selling. I'll watch you with the first customer to make sure you've got it.

Scout 1:   Pentholls.

Scout 2:   You need to be more enthusiastic!

Scout 3 enters the stage.

Scout 1:   Pentholls, Pentholls.

Scout 3:   How much for the Pencils?

Scout 1:   Pentholls, pentholls.

Scout 3:   I know pencils, how much?

Scout 1:   Pentholls, pentholls.

Scout 3:   Never mind. *Scout 3 walks away.*

Scout 2:   No, no, no! When someone asks you how much for the pencils you tell them one for a nickel, two for a dime and 5 for a quarter.

Scout 1:   Two for a nickel, a dime for a quarter.

Scout 2:   No, no. One for a nickel, two for a dime and 5 for a quarter.

Scout 1:   Two for a nickel, 3 for a dime a bunch for a quarter.

Scout 2:   You've more or less got it. Now if someone asks you why they should buy your pencils, you say, if you don't somebody else will.

Scout 1:   If you don't, somebody else will.

Scout 2:   Very good. Now go out there and give it another try.

Scout 2 disappears and a fourth Scout enters. Scout 1 runs to him shouting and waving his hands.

Scout 1:   Pentholls!!!, pentholls!!!

Scout 4:   Get away from me you jerk. How many people have you done this to anyway?

Scout 1: Two, three, five.

Scout 4:   You're really asking for a punch in the mouth stupid.

Scout 1:   If you don't, somebody else will.

Scout 4 punches Scout 1 and he falls to the ground. The end.

Dying of Thirst

Participants: 3.
Props: Glass of Water and a comb.

An empty glass of water is placed in the center of the stage. A Scout crawls along the floor crying for water. He dies dramatically before reaching the glass. A second Scout acts the same way and dies after getting a little closer to the glass than the first. A third Scout comes along acting very much like the first two. This Scout struggles dramatically and gets to the point just in front of the glass. At that point, he reaches into his pocket, grabs a comb, sticks it in the glass of water, combs his hair, sighs with relief and exits the stage.

Walk the Plank

Participants: 3 to 7.
Props: A board and optionally pirate garb.

The skit begins with the captain of a pirate ship saying "Today, someone is going to walk the plank." Other scouts in the area pretend to be completing chores associated with working on a ship (swabbing the deck, raising sails, etc.). The Captain approaches each of the other scouts telling them that today they need to walk the plank. Each shudders in fear and then comes up with a silly reason why they can't walk the plank today. The came accepts these excuses by saying "well all right" and then approaches the next scout in the group. Finally the captain approaches the last scout and says, "You're going to walk the plank." The final scout says, "OK, and he walks to the side of the stage and returns pulling a board on a rope." He is "walking the plank."

The Four Seasons

Participants: 3 plus 2 volunteers.
Props: none.

The narrator begins by asking four volunteers to participate. Each volunteer is assigned a role in the skit; roles include a tree, a bird, a babbling brook and the trees lifeblood, the sap. Generally two of the volunteers are "plants" who know in advance their roles as the tree and the bird. The brook and the sap are then left to follow the careful instruction of the narrator. Each of the participants acts out their assigned role. For example, the tree raises his arms to signifying leaves growing in the spring. He lowers his arms in the fall.

Narrator: To the babbling brook - you need to babble.
Brook: Babble, babble, babble....

Narrator: In the Spring the leaves come out on the trees(the tree raises his arms above his head), the birds begin to sing(bird - chirp, chirp, chirp), the brook begins to babble rapidly(brook starts babbling faster), and the sap, which provides valuable nutrients to the tree, begins to run(sap starts running).

The narrator continues to describe activities throughout summer and fall, and throughout this narration, the sap's job is to continue running at various paces. In the winter, the dialog ends with a narration that goes something like this: In the winter the brook freezes and stops babbling(babbling stops). The birds are gone and the trees seem lifeless and without motion. But through it all there is still some activity, for you see, the sap keeps running.

Mmm Good

Participants: 4.
Props: A large pot and several spoons.   A mop makes this skit more effective.
Announcer: The following skit takes places in the dining hall.
Scout 1: Boy this sure is good soup.
Scout 2: Yeah, this is the best food we've had at camp all week.
Cook: *(carrying mop)* What are you two doing? Get those spoons out of my mop water.

The Fortune Teller

Participants: 5 plus 1 volunteer.
Props: 3 dollar bills.

MC: I'd now like to introduce the amazing Felix who can tell your fortune simply by smelling your shoe.
Felix: Thank you, Thank you. Who would like to be my first volunteer. *(Felix selects a "plant" from the audience, the Scout comes forward takes off his shoe and hands it to Felix. Felix smells the shoe and predicts that a Scout leader will give him a dollar. A nearby Scout leader walks over and hands him a dollar.)*
Scout 1:   Wow! Thanks a lot.
Felix: Who will be my next volunteer? *(Felix selects a "plant" from the audience, the Scout come forward takes off his shoe and hands it to Felix. Felix smells the shoe and predicts that a Scout leader will give him two dollars. A nearby Scout leader walks over and hands him two dollars).*
Scout 2:   Wow! Thanks a lot.
Felix: Who will be my next volunteer? *(This time Felix selects an unsuspecting victim. The victim takes off his shoe and hands it to Felix. Felix throws the shoe to the back of the audience and says)*
           I predict you will go for a long walk.

13

Gathering of the Nuts

Participants: 1 plus volunteers.
Props: None.

Version 1

Announcer: Andre, the famous French impressionist painter, is here to create a living portrait of nature's beauty at tonight's campfire.

(It helps to have Andre portrayed by someone flamboyant, with an overdone French accent).

Andre: Thank you, thank you very much everyone. To create this portrait I will need help from you, our lovely audience. First I will need some trees *(volunteers come forward and are positioned as trees)*. Next, I will need some birds *(volunteer birds are instructed to flap their wings among the trees)*. Eventually, hopping bunnies and a babbling brook are added with volunteers acting out these roles. Andre then turns to the audience and speaks. Another magnificent masterpiece is completed, I call this portrait, "The Gathering of the Nuts."

Version 2

Participants: No limit.
Props: None.

For this skit, the MC announces that the "Squirrel Patrol" will be performing the next skit. Members from the patrol walk around the crowd and select volunteers to help them with their skit. The volunteers are brought to the front of the campfire and members of the Squirrel Patrol sit down. The announcer comes forward and says lets give the Squirrel Patrol a big hand for that last skit which they like to call, "The Gathering of the Nuts."

Scout Socks

Participants: 4.
Props: Several pairs of socks.

The Scout leader drops a pile of socks on the ground and invites three Scouts to come up and take some.

Scout 1:	I need three pair.
Leader:	How come?
Scout 1:	I only do laundry every three days.
Leader:	Okay, here you go.
Scout 2:	I need seven pair.
Leader:	Seven pair? Why?
Scout 2:	One for Monday, one for Tuesday, Wednesday, Thursday, Friday, Saturday and Sunday.
Leader:	Okay, here you go.
Scout 3:	I need twelve pair.
Leader:	Twelve pair, that's ridiculous. What do you need twelve pair for?
Scout 3:	*(Counting on Fingers)* Well there's January, February, March....

Sock Exchange

Participants: Minimum of 4.
Props: None.

A group of Scouts march in single file. Their leader announces, "I know its been a long hike, and you guys are tired. Before you set up camp, I've got some good news and some bad news to tell you. The good news is after all these weeks of hiking, leadership says you can have a change of socks." *(The Scouts cheer).* "The bad news is, John is changing with Peter, Albert is changing with Harry......"

Lobster Tails

Participants: 3.
Props: A plate and a book.

Three Scouts are needed for this skit. Two Scouts walk into a restaurant and a waiter comes in to take their order. "I'll have a steak," the first Scout says, and the second Scout orders a lobster tail. The waiter returns with one plate and a book. He gives the plate to the first Scout, then sits next to the second and begins to read. "Once upon a time there was a little lobster.....".

This skit can be worked into a set of restaurant sketches which can include lines from the **Fly in My Soup** section.

There's a Fly in My Soup

Participants: 2 minimum.
Props: None.

For this skit to be effective you really need to keep it moving. This skit can be done alone or it can be worked into a series of restaurant skits which might include **Lobster Tails** or **Mmm Good**.

Patron:	Do you serve crab?
Waiter:	Sit down, we serve anyone.
Patron:	Waiter, there's a fly in my soup.
Waiter:	Quiet or everyone will want one.
Patron:	What's this fly doing in my soup?
Waiter:	It looks like he's doing the backstroke.
Patron:	Waiter there's a fly in my soup.
Waiter:	It's the rotting meat that attracts them.
Patron:	What's this fly doing in my soup?
Waiter:	Playing water polo.
Patron:	Waiter, there's a fly in my soup.
Waiter:	What's the big deal. He won't eat much.
Patron:	What's this fly doing in my alphabet soup?
Waiter:	Learning to read.
Patron:	This food isn't fit for a pig.
Waiter:	Sorry I'll bring you some that is.

Panther Tracks

Participants: 2.
Props: None.

Scout 1: *(pointing)* Hey look! Animal tracks. I wonder what kind they are?
Scout 2: They are obviously cat tracks. BIIGGG cat tracks.
Scout 1: You think they're from a mountain lion?
Scout 2: I don't know. Let's take a closer look.

Both Scouts get on their knees

Scout 1: Well, what do you think?

Scout 2: There's no doubt about it. Those are panther tracks.

Scout 1: Panther tracks? How can you be so sure?

Scout 2: Do you see the bottom of this track. There is an ant squished at the bottom. And there's one in this track too. The animal that made these tracks was purposely stepping on ants as he walked.

Scout 1: O.K., I'll grant you this animal likes to squish ants, but how can you be so sure this cat is a panther?

Scout 2: Why that's easy. *(pointing to the ground as he talks)* Just look at the pattern.   DEAD-ANT, DEAD-ANT, DEAD-ANT, DEAD-ANT, DEAD-ANT*(Say this to the tune of the pink panther theme)*.

Suckers on the Line

This skit has no less than 20 variations, here are three of the more popular versions.

Version 1

Participants: 2 plus 3 volunteers.
Props: None.

Scout 1:   *(Pretends to dial a phone, then makes ringing sound)*

Scout 2:   *(Pretends to pick up phone)* Hello.

Scout 1:   Jim is that you?

Scout 2:   I can hardly hear you.

Scout 2 asks for a volunteer to hold up the phone line. The same type of dialog continues until three or more volunteers are brought forward. The final dialog goes something like this.

Scout 2: Well, that's better. Now I can hear you.

Scout 1: So Jim, what have you been up to?

Scout 2: I went fishing today.

Scout 1: No kidding. Any luck.

Scout 2: Yeah, I caught three suckers on the line!

18

Version 2

Participants: 2 plus 2 volunteers.
Props: A pole and a blanket.

A candy store owner enters carrying a long pole and a blanket. He asks two volunteers from the audience to hold the pole, and then he drapes the blanket over it, explaining that inside is his candy store. A customer comes in and asks for every conceivable type of candy. The owner explains that he is out of that kind. Exasperated, the customer finally says, "Well then, what do you have?" The owner pulls off the blanket and replies, "Just two suckers on a stick."

Version 3

Participants: 2 plus unlimited volunteers.
Props: A rope.

Two people walk on stage with a long rope stretched between them. One of the Scouts explains that he is a fisherman, the other explains that he runs the local fish market. They attempt to contact each other by phone, and the fisherman acts as if he can't hear the fish market manager. Volunteers are brought forward to hold the rope. When several volunteers are up holding the rope they can finally hear each other. The fisherman says that he doesn't have any salmon, but he did catch a bunch of suckers on the line.

Covered Wagon

Participants: 2 plus volunteers.
Props: None.
One Scout acts as a covered wagon; he is positioned at the front of the audience on his hands and knees.   The other Scout is the wagon driver. The wagon driver uses the following monologue:

Darn, my wagon wheel is broken. I need a volunteer to hold it on the wagon. *(The driver selects a volunteer who stands next to one of the wagon wheels)*

Darn it this wagon still won't go. Now the other wheel is loose. I need another volunteer to hold this wheel on the wagon. *(The driver selects another volunteer who stands next on the other side of the "wagon").*

There that did it. Now it will work. All I needed was a couple of nuts to hold on the wheels.

A Day at Summer Camp

Participants: 4 minimum.
Props: Sleeping Bags, a bag of M & M's, a deck of cards.

This skit features a narrator and two Scouts. The narrator reads a sugary story about what life at summer camp is like. The Scouts then act out the complete opposite of what the narrator says. The narrator's piece follows in plain text, examples of what the Scouts might do follow in italics.

You jump out of bed to the excitement of another day at camp. *The Scouts slowly get out of their sleeping bags and say, Oh no not another rainy day.*   The cook sounds off, "Come and get it", and you enjoy a hot hearty breakfast. *Scouts open up a bag of M & M's and begin eating.* After breakfast there's work to be done, you tidily re-organize your tent, *Scouts roll there sleeping bags* into a big mess, and help clean up the camp area. *Scouts throw the empty bag of M & M's and other trash from their tent on the ground.* You're now ready for the day's adventure. What will it be today? A hike along a wilderness trail? Knot tying sessions? Exploring a cave, canoeing or swimming? *One of the Scouts says, "Do you want to play poker?" and they sit down to play cards.* So much to do, yet so little time. Afternoon at camp has a way of rocketing by. So many things to do, so little time. *Scouts say, "I'm bored, there's nothing to do here." A second Scout says, "you could sit here and watch me play solitaire. The second Scout does.* There's the rifle range, archery practice; you could build a signal tower, or go for another swim. Supper is probably the eating highlight of the day. But at Scout camp it is even much more than that, it is a chance for Scouts to share in good fellowship. *A fight breaks out among the Scouts.* Hurry now! Supper's over and it's time to enjoy the campfire. *Scouts slowly walk to the campfire.* There's fun galore as you gaze into the campfire and feel the strong bonds of comradeship that's pulling you and your brother Scouts together. *One Scout pushes another away from him.* After the campfire Scouts return to their tents. Happy dreams! Tomorrow is another day full of excitement and surprises.

Fire Safety Officer

Participants: 2.
Props: A bucket of water. Optional: raincoat or firemen's gear.

The campfire begins with the MC introducing the Fire Safety Officer. The Fire Safety Officer comes out holding a bucket of water as the MC discusses the importance of having water near a fire. The Fire Safety Officer's only job is to make sure that the campfire does not get out of control. The more serious the MC can be in portraying the danger of fire, the better this routine works. If the Fire Safety Officer can wear a raincoat, firemen's suit or uniform, it will make him easier to identify later in the evening. The Fire Safety Officer goes over and stands to the side and the MC goes on with the program.

Later in the program victims are selected to assist in a variety of skits. **The Firing Squad** skit is performed and when someone yells fire, the Fire Safety Officer runs over and throws water on the firing squad. During **I Don't Know How or Leaky Submarine**, the Fire Safety Officer can douse the Scout who says "Fire torpedo one." **Dying of Thirst** can be performed and when the Scout crawls on the ground crying water, the Fire Safety Officer runs out and throws water on the crawling Scout. Needless to say the Fire Safety Officer can have a busy night running out and throwing water every time he hears the "keywords" fire or water.

Radio Skit

Participants: 6.
Props: A boom box or large radio.

This skit requires six Scouts. (or a few Scouts that can very effectively change their voices). One Scout is seated with a large radio turning the dial hoping to find some good music. He stops and listens to each station, finding a cooking show, a football game, the children's story hour and a detective story. The humor in this skit lies in the transition from one program to the next. This skit can be especially funny if Scouts try to sound like a famous cooking show host, football announcer, etc.

Gangster:	. . . . . .Man, what a jerk you are! What don't you drop dead here and now and save me the trouble of putting this slug through your hide? Steal my girl, will ya? There's only one thing that can save you now pal, only one thing that can save you now. . . . . .
Scout:	. . . .The Boy {Girl} Scouts of America. . .
Cooking show:	. . . . . .and ladies, I think you'll agree that that's a beautiful ham, not a speck of fat on it. And

	that's the way it should be, lean and juicy and so full of. . . . . .
Football game:	. . . . . .unnecessary roughness. So it's a 15 yard penalty pushing the Jets all the way back to their own 12 yard line. Ut, oh, there's a big argument with the official, the Jet's captain is shouting up a storm and I can imagine what the official is saying to the captain. . . . . .
Story hour:	. . . . ."My, what a big mouth you have, grandmother!" And at that moment, the wolf threw off the grandmother's clothes and said, "All the better to eat you with, my dear." Then Little Red Riding Hood cried, "Save me, oh, who will save me?"
Scout:	.. . .The Boy {Girl} Scouts of America. . .
Football game:	. . . . .and boy are they confused! It looks like he's going to pass on this play. The quarterback launches a long, high wobbling one going way down field. Wow, it looks like its heading straight for the. . . .
Cooking show:	. . . .automatic electric waffle iron and sandwich toaster. Of course if you remove the waffle or sandwich too soon or too late it will be. . . . . .
Football game:	. . . . .thrown for a big loss! Too bad; that big defensive end from South Bend rose up and said, "Nothing doin' boys, its mine." Yes sir, those Jets are one terrific team, I tell ya. For my money, there's only one outfit in the country that could take the Jets and that's. . . . . .
Scout:	.. . .The Boy Scouts of America!!. Yes, just think, about the great time you'll have camping this summer. Lot's of hiking and swimming and plenty of great food. And in the evening, gazing into the campfire with no companion but the wind, the stars, and. . . . .
Story hour:	. . . . . ."Little Red Riding Hood. Yes children Little Red Riding Hood safe and sound. As for the wolf. . . . . .

23

Football game:	. . . . .I'm afraid he'll never play football again. He's definitely down and out, he's played his last song. There's a time-out on the field, so let's remind everyone that this broadcast is brought to you by Sharp, the razor whiskers are afraid of. With Sharp, the sharpest razors in the world. . . . .
Gangster:	. . . . . .you can cut your throat for all I care, you twisted jerk. What's the matter? Ya scared? Whatcha scared-a pal? Whatcha scared-a? What's a big strong guy like you afraid of?. . . . . .
Scout:	.. . .The Boy Scouts of America. . .

North by Northwest

Participants: 4 minimum.
Props: None.

A group of Scouts sit along the side of the stage and a movie director approaches them. He is casting a new film and he needs someone to act as a stand in. He asks this group of Scouts if anyone would like to volunteer. One Scout excitedly jumps up and down and says, choose me, choose me. The director make a concerted effort to choose someone else. He pretends not to notice this Scout and tries to look past him for other volunteers. The other Scouts appear disinterested and finally, very reluctantly, the director chooses the enthusiastic Scout.

The director next explains the part to the Scout who was selected as the "Stand-in". The dialog follows:

Director:	Okay now, your part is very simple. You barge in with important news for the captain. You say to him, "Captain, Captain, our ship is sinking, we've hit an iceberg." When the captain asks you how far from land we are, you tell him five nautical miles. Finally,

	when he asks you what direction we're headed, answer north by northwest. Do you have it?
Stand-in:	Yeah, yeah, yeah, I've got it.
Director:	Okay everyone take your positions .....Action.
Stand-in:	Captain, Captain, your ship is stinking.
Director:	Cut, cut, cut. No, no, no, your line is captain, captain your ship is sinking; sinking, got it?
Stand-in:	Yeah, yeah, yeah, I've got it.
Director:	Okay, action.
Stand-in:	Captain, Captain, your ship is sinking. We've hit an ice cube.
Director:	Cut, cut, cut. No, no, you idiot we've hit an iceberg. That's an ICEBERG. Do you think you have it?
Stand-in:	Yeah, yeah, yeah, I've got it.
Director:	Okay, action.
Stand-in:	Captain, Captain, your ship is sinking. We've hit an iceberg.
Captain:	How far off land are we?
Stand-in:	Five naked models.
Director:	Cuuuttttt. Its five nautical miles, not five naked models. Do you think you can remember your lines this time?
Stand-in:	Yeah, yeah, yeah, I've got it.
Director:	Okay, action.
Stand-in:	Captain, Captain, your ship is sinking. We've hit an iceberg.
Captain:	How far off land are we?
Stand-in:	Five nautical miles.
Captain:	What direction are we headed?
Stand-in:	Straight down.
Director:	CCUUUTTTTTTT. *Director chases stand-in off stage. The end.*

The Restaurant

Participants: 2 minimum plus volunteers.
Props: Glasses of water.

The narrator initiates this skit by asking for a volunteer. This volunteer is instructed to get on his hands and knees to serve as a bar or table. Next, additional volunteers are asked to act as customers at a restaurant. The customers are instructed to sit next to the table and they are told to converse while the waiter offers them a drink. The waiter then places two water glasses on the table, (the back of the first volunteer) while the customers are chatting. The skit ends when the customers are told the restaurant is closed, and it is time to leave. The "table" is left with the job of trying to get up without spilling water on his back.

The World's Greatest Spitter

Participants: 3 minimum.
Props: A bucket of water.

This skit requires several Scouts, a spitter, a catcher and some "plants" who remain in the audience. A bucket half filled with water is left on stage.

A Scout, the spitter, walks on stage and proclaims that he is the greatest spitter in the world. He brags about his ability, and claims that he can spit farther than any other living being. "Plants" in the audience challenge the spitter to prove it, saying they do not believe him.

The spitter agrees to take up the challenge and asks for a volunteer to assist him. He selects the catcher who acts as if he expects to be the victim.

The spitter explains that he will stand 10 feet away from the catcher, and that he will spit directly into the bucket, demonstrating his distance and accuracy. The catcher complains saying, "You'd better not hit me with your spit!" "You just need to make sure you hold the bucket still," the spitter replies.

The spitter pretends to spit and the catcher pretends to catch the spit tapping the bottom of the bucket as if the spit made noise as it hit the can." The spitter hams it up and takes a huge bow.

The "plants" in the audience act unimpressed claiming "Anyone could do that." So the spitter responds by repeating his feat from several distances. At last the spitter claims he will prove he is the greatest by spitting completely around the world. He pretends to perform that feat and takes an even bigger bow.

The "plants" complain that the spitter is a fake and they yell for him to get off the stage. They say no one could spit around the world. The spitter says that he can prove that he did it. With that he says to the catcher, "Show them."

The Catcher then throws the bucket of water on the crowd.

Saint Peter

Participants: 4.
Props: None.

A Scout is introduced as Saint Peter who is guarding the pearly gates to heaven. A group of three Scouts arrive at the pearly gates each hoping to get into heaven.

Scout 1:	Saint Peter can I go into heaven?
Saint Peter:	First you need to tell me how you suffered on earth.
Scout 1:	I went on a long hike and got blisters on my feet.
Saint Peter:	I'm sorry, you haven't suffered enough, you can't enter.
	(Scout 1 walks away, disappointed)
Scout 2:	Saint Peter can I go into heaven?
Saint Peter:	Tell me how you suffered on earth.
Scout 2:	I spent a week eating camp food.
Saint Peter:	I'm sorry, you haven't suffered enough, you can't enter.
	(Scout 2 walks away, disappointed)
Scout 3:	Saint Peter can I go into heaven?
Saint Peter:	How did you suffer?.
Scout 3:	I was in (pick the name of someone with a sense of humor) (troop, campsite, patrol, etc.)
Saint Peter:	Welcome to Heaven!!!

Thar's A Bear

Participants: 2 plus volunteers.
Props: None.

The skitleader selects several volunteers from the audience who are told to mimic the actions of the skitleader. It may be beneficial to have the second Scout be in on the skit so that each subsequent Scout knows what to do. However, you can just spring this trick on several unsuspecting victims, if you explain it well enough. The volunteers line up side by side facing the audience. The Skitleader begins, then pairs of Scouts in the line repeat the following dialog and actions. The skitleader purposely mispronounces his words; volunteers are instructed to mimic the skit leaders pronunciation. Mispronunciation is important, it adds a great deal to the skit.

Skitleader: There's a Bar(Bear).
Scout 1: Whar?(Where?).
Skitleader: Over Thar(There)
Skitleader points his right arm across his body and remains in this position.
Scout 1: Over Thar?(There?)
Skitleader: Over Thar(There)

Scout 1: There's a Bar(Bear).
Scout 2: Whar?(Where?).
Scout 1: Over Thar(There)
Scout 1 maintains his action pointing his right arm across his body.
Scout 2:   Over Thar?(There?)
Scout 2 points his right arm across his body and remains in this position.
Scout 1:   Over Thar(There).

Scout 2 and Scout 3 repeat this exchange, Scout 3 and Scout 4, etc., until all volunteers are standing with one arm pointed across their body. The Skitleader starts again, this time pointing with the left arm across his body, while maintaining the action of pointing his right arm across his body. The dialog and actions are repeated all the way down the line. Next the Skitleader lifts his right leg and points it to the left and again all Scouts follow his action while continuing to hold their crossed arms pointed in opposite directions. One final time the Skitleader begins, this time pointing his head left toward the bear, with all the volunteers following suite. At this point all the volunteers have reached the point of being quite silly, and quite off balance as each is standing on one leg with arms crossed and head tilted. The skitleader then pushes the first Scout in the line and the entire group will fall over like dominoes. You have no idea how funny this skit can be until you've seen it performed.

The Important Meeting

Participants: 4 minimum.
Props: Toy microphone (optional).

The important meeting skit can incorporate up to 10 Scouts. Additionally, you can use this skit to introduce shy Scouts to participating in skits without requiring them to take a major role. The skit begins with some number of Scouts seated around a table in a serious discussion. Some Scouts may be taking notes, others may be pretending to be in passionate and animated discussions. A narrator speaks over the committee and introduces himself as a television reporter. In hushed tones the narrator talks about these individuals coming together to help make some very important decisions.

The narrator completes his role by saying something like "let's listen in and hear what these committee members have to say." The group quiets down and a committee chairman stands up and says in a loud voice, "Then its decided. We'll have two large pizzas, one with pepperoni, the other with sausage."

The committee members cheer in agreement.

Napoleon's Farewell Address

Participants: 5 minimum.
Props: None.

The Narrator sets the stage for a very moving moment where Napoleon addresses his troops after their defeat in the battle of Waterloo. "Imagine thousands of exhausted men, road weary from months away from home, battle fatigued and distraught over the loss of comrades. What words of encouragement does Napoleon have for these men? Let's listen to the words of his immortal farewell address....."

Another Scout walks forward, slowly and quietly. When he reaches the center of the stage, he stops very deliberately, places his right hand under the breast of his Scout uniform and says, "Farewell Troops."

Variations
The Narrator talks of the moving speech George Washington gave when he completed his presidency. A Scout walks forward and simply says "Farewell." The Narrator can follow-up by asking the Scouts if they know why George Washington's address was important. The answer is, of course, so that they would know where to deliver his mail.

Listen!
Participants: 2.
Props: None.

A Scout sits at the center of the stage with his ear to the ground, listening intently. Another Scout walks on stage watching the first Scout. After a minute he, too, places his ear to the ground and listens intently. Finally, the second Scout says, "I don't hear anything." The first Scout replies, "I know, it's been like this all day."

The Secret Papers

Participants: 4 minimum.
Props: None.

This Skit can also be done as the special papers, royal papers or the important papers. The main idea is that some person of authority, who in this example we will call the king, calls in his assistants and tells them that he urgently needs the secret papers. Different assistants return one at a time with various papers which the person of authority discards. As each assistant returns with the wrong "secret papers" the king becomes more and more agitated, demanding in stronger and stronger terms that his less than intelligent assistants bring him his secret papers. The skit concludes when an assistant supplies the king with a roll of toilet paper and this assistant is praised by the king.

Variations:
Substitute the president or a business executive for the king.
Have the assistant who supplies the secret papers be a court jester who is knighted for supplying the secret papers.
Have each servant who does not get the correct secret papers executed for their incompetence.

The Trained Flea

Participants: 2.
Props: None.

A Scout acts as a flea trainer and comes forward and explains the various tricks his flea Herman is performing. After several tricks, Herman jumps into the audience. A Scout comes forward claiming to have a flea in his hair. The flea trainer examines the Scout's head and says, "That's not Herman!"

Telephone Magic

Participants: 4 minimum.

Props: *Banana, neckerchief, an old cap, a cup, eggs and a magic wand.*

All props are placed on a table in the front of the room. The MC comes forward and announces that tonight's magic show has to be canceled because the magician cannot make it. A phone rings and the MC pretends to be in a conversation with the magician who is off stage. The magician has agreed to have a volunteer from the audience perform his tricks by following his telephone instructions. The MC selects a volunteer who is really a "Plant" who is part of the act. The volunteer comes forward and acts like he does not understand the directions. He picks up the phone and begins to follow the magician's instructions which are audible to the entire group.

Magician: Take the neckerchief from the table.
Volunteer: Duh, aaahh, which one is the neckerchief?
Magician: You know, its like a handkerchief.
Volunteer: Hinkerchiff?
Magician: What are you some kind of fool? Handkerchief, it's like a bandanna.
Volunteer: Banana, why didn't you say so. I've got it right here. *Volunteer picks up the banana.*
Magician: Okay, take the bandanna and fold it in half.
Volunteer: Okay. *Volunteer breaks the banana in half.*
Magician: Now make a fist and stuff the bandanna in your fist.
Volunteer: *Volunteer stuffs the banana in his fist.*
Magician: Now say the magic words, "Abra ca dabra", and the bandanna will be gone.
Volunteer: Da Crabra *Volunteer opens his fist to reveal a soggy banana.*
Magician: For our next trick grab the cup.
Volunteer: Okay, I've got the cap.
Magician: Break two eggs into the cup.

33

Volunteer:	Volunteer breaks some number of eggs in the cap but miscounts Like 1, 4, 2.
Magician:	Now beat the eggs with the magic fork.
	Volunteer strikes the cap several times with the fork like you would beat someone with a club.
Magician:	Now place the magic hat on your head.
	Volunteer places the hat on his head as eggs drips onto his face.
Magician:	Now wave the magic wand over the cup and say the magic words, abra ca dabra. Turn the cup over and it will be empty. The empty cup is turned over.

The MC says lets give a big round of applause for our volunteer. He then reminds Scouts not to be too quick to volunteer during skits or they can end up with egg on their face.

Down South Pickin' Cotton

Participants: 4.
Props: Boom box, jacket, sneakers and a towel.

Scout 1 is standing in the middle of the stage as several other Scouts walk by one at a time.

A Scout walks by carrying a boom box
Scout 1: Hey where did you get that great stereo?
Scout 2: Down south pickin' cotton.
A Scout walks by wearing a jacket
Scout 1: Where'd you get that great jacket?
Scout 3: Down south pickin' cotton.
A Scout walks by wearing sneakers
Scout 1: Where'd you get those cool sneakers?
Scout 3: Down south pickin' cotton.
A Scout walks by limping, and beat up wearing nothing but a towel.
Scout 1: What happened to you?
Scout 4: I'm Cotton.

I Don't Know How

Participants: 4 or 5.
Props: None.

A group of Scouts (usually four) are standing in line, one behind the other. Messages are passed up and down the line with the captain, who is first issuing the commands, and the last Scout answering each command with, "I don't know how."

Captain: Fire torpedo one.
Scout 2: Fire torpedo one.
Scout 3: Fire torpedo one.
Scout 4: I don't know how.
Scout 3: He doesn't know how.
Scout 2: He doesn't know how.
Scout 1: Push de button.
Scout 2: Push de button.
Scout 3: Push de button.
Scout 4: *pretends to push a button*
Captain: Missed! Fire torpedo two.
Scout 2: Fire torpedo two.
Scout 3: Fire torpedo two.
Scout 4: I don't know how.
Scout 3: He doesn't know how.
Scout 2: He doesn't know how.
Scout 1: Push de button.
Scout 2: Push de button.
Scout 3: Push de button.
Scout 4: *pretends to push a button*

This routine is done a third time. Finally, the Captain says, if we miss this time we're all going to kill ourselves.

Captain: Missed! Fire torpedo four.
Scout 2: Fire torpedo four.

Scout 3: Fire torpedo four.
Scout 4: I don't know how.
Scout 3: He doesn't know how.
Scout 2: He doesn't know how.
Scout 1: Push de button.
Scout 2: Push de button.
Scout 3: Push de button.
Scout 4: *pretends to push a button.*
Captain: Missed! *Captain shoots himself.*
Scout 2: *picks up gun and shoots himself.*
Scout 3: *picks up gun and shoots himself.*
Scout 4: *picks up gun and says,* I don't know how.

The Incredible Enlarging Machine

Participants: 2 plus multiple volunteers.
Props: Backdrop, bucket of water and large and small objects.

This skit requires small and large versions of objects. If you didn't bring props on your campout, you can always use small and large version of pots, rope, logs etc. Set up a large backdrop using a sheet, sleeping bag or blanket. A Scout hides behind this blanket with the large props and a bucket of water. The narrator is in front of the blanket with the small objects.

Narrator: I have developed the world's first enlarging machine. I can take any object and make it bigger. I will need a few volunteers to help me demonstrate how the machine works.

Volunteers are called forward. The Narrator hands them small objects and they throw them behind the blanket. Larger versions are tossed out by the hidden Scout. The last volunteer is the victim. The Narrator hands the victim a cup filled with water. He whispers in the victims ear that there is really a Scout behind the blanket and the trick is to walk to the edge of the blanket and to douse the Scout behind the curtain with the cup of water. As the victim does this, the Scout behind the curtain douses the victim with a bucket of water.

Doctor, Doctor!

Participants: 2 minimum.
Props: None.

For this skit to be effective you really need to keep it moving. This can be done by having a series of Scouts walk on stage back to back as doctor and patient. Or the skit can be done by the same two Scouts appearing quickly between each skit.

Patient: Doctor, I'm scared. This is my first operation.
Doctor: I know just how you feel. You're my first patient.

Patient: Doctor, do you think I'll kick the bucket?
Doctor: No, but you do look a little pail.
Patient: Seriously Doctor, am I going to die.
Doctor: That's the last thing you'll do.

Patient: Doctor, doctor, everyone says I'm a bell.
Doctor: Take two aspirins and give me a ring in the morning.

Patient: Doctor, can I sleep in my contact lenses?
Doctor: No, your feet would stick out.

Patient: Doctor, doctor, I feel like a set of drapes.
Doctor: Pull yourself together.

Patient: Doctor, doctor, I feel like a pack of cards
Doctor: Quiet, I'll deal with you later.

Patient: Doctor, doctor, everyone keeps ignoring me.
Doctor: Next!

Patient: Doctor, do you think that raw oysters are healthy?
Doctor: I never met one that was sick.

Patient: Doctor, you've got to help me. I keep thinking I'm invisible.
Doctor: Who said that?

Patient: Doctor, doctor, I'm afraid I'm a Kleptomaniac.
Doctor: Are you taking anything for it?

Patient: Doctor, doctor, I think I'm suffering from amnesia.
Doctor: How long have you had it?
Patient: Had what?

Doctor: You've got too much snew growing on your arms.
Patient: What's snew?
Doctor: Not much, what's new with you?

J. C. Penney

Participants: 4.
Props: A pair of jeans, a jacket, sneakers and a towel.

Scout 1 is standing in the middle of the stage as several other Scouts walk by one at a time.

A Scout walks by wearing jeans.
Scout 1:   Hey, where did you get those great jeans?
Scout 2:   J. C. Penney.
A Scout walks by wearing a jacket.
Scout 1:   Where'd you get that great jacket?
Scout 3:   J. C. Penney.
A Scout walks by wearing sneakers.
Scout 1:   Where'd you get those cool sneakers?
Scout 3:   J. C. Penney.
A Scout walks by wearing nothing but a towel.
Scout 1:   Who are you?
Scout 4:   J. C. Penney.

Variations
This skit can also be done as L. L. Bean or Montgomery Ward.

The Lost Lollipop

Participants: 2.
Props: A blanket.

This skit requires 2 Scouts, one plays the part of a Scout who has lost his lollipop, the other plays the role of a monk from an eastern religion. Optionally, the monk can be dressed in a blanket, symbolizing a monk's robes.

Scout: *Sobbing* I've lost my yummy little red lollipop.

Monk: *Walks in with hands together chanting ummmm...he stops and asks :*
What's the matter my child?

Scout: Weren't you listening? I've lost my yummy little red lollipop.

Monk: Well, have you looked for it?

Scout: I've looked and I've looked, but I just can't seem to find my yummy little red lollipop.

Monk: When your eyes fail you, you must reach for a higher consciousness. If you chant loud enough, the location of your yummy little red lollipop will be revealed to you.

Scout: Chant?

Monk: Yes, chant. Just keep repeating the phrase, my yummy little red lollipop, my yummy little red lollipop.....

Scout: My yummy little red lollipop, my yummy little red lollipop, my yummy little red lollipop..... it's not working.

Monk: Perhaps you chant too softly. *Turning to the audience* Maybe you can help. Just repeat after me. My yummy little red lollipop, my yummy little red lollipop.....*The monk gets the whole audience loudly repeating the phrase. He then turns back to the Scout.* Did it work?

Scout: *Very loudly* No, but I did find a whole lot of suckers!

Oh-Wa Ta-Foo Li-Am

Participants: No limit.
Props: None.

In many troops, this routine was reserved for introducing new Scouts to campfires. Since this skit cannot be performed on the same Scout twice, it should be used only occasionally, at small troop settings. Scouts are called forward and are told to kneel in front of the campfire. Next, they are instructed to raise their arms above their head. In a repetitive motion they should touch the ground in front of them with their hands and then raise them above their heads again. This action fans the fire, and the fire god likes it a lot. While acting in this way, Scouts must repeat the fire god's words of worship, Oh-Wa Ta-Foo Li-am . These words should be repeated slowly at first, with the words in each successive chant faster and closer together. When a Scout becomes enlightened to the meaning of the fire god's words, they are instructed to whisper the meaning to the MC. The MC tells the Scouts who understand the phrase to sit down. Hopefully before too long all Scouts will understand that they are repeating, "Oh What a Fool I am."
Variations
Other phrases such as Oh-Wa Ta-Gu Si-Am, or Oh-Wa Ta-Nas Si-Am may be used instead.

The Little Lost Sheep

Participants: 4 minimum.
Props: None.

The MC introduces what is arguably the top singing patrol in the United States. Their many awards include the Fulbright songster award and the Alto choir prize. After a big build up, the patrol marches forward as the MC announces their number, "The Lost Little Sheep." On the count of three the patrol sings one word "Baaaa-aaa-aa-a".

Lincoln Memorial

Participants: 3.
Props: A container.

A Scout sits motionless while an announcer and a Doctor stand beside the Scout:

Announcer: We are standing here at the Lincoln Memorial where Dr. Van Guildersmith is about to test his latest invention which transforms calcium into living tissue. He hopes to bring Abraham Lincoln back to life so we can gain some valuable insight into the thinking of this tremendously popular man.

The Doctor pretends to pour the substance on the Scout who is acting as the statue. The statue moves and begins to speak.

Statue: Four Score and Seven Years ago...
Doctor: Mr. Lincoln, Mr. Lincoln.
Statue: Where am I?
Doctor: I have brought you back to life so you could share with us your incredible insight.
Statue: I see.
Doctor: Let me begin by asking you if there was one thing you wished you had done when you were alive what would it be?
Statue: Well, I wish I had used my gun more.
Doctor: Used your gun more? Mr. Lincoln, I thought you were a man of peace.
Statue: I am, but if I had it to do all over again I would have killed every pigeon within 500 miles of Washington...

Igor

Participants: 5 minimum.
Props: None.

A mad scientist has created a monster named Igor. With pride the scientist talks about how he can conquer the world with the help of Igor who he has taught to obey three different commands. Scouts come to the mad scientist's door under different pretenses, to sell magazines, Girl Scout cookies, Mary Kay cosmetics, etc. Each time the mad scientist disposes of them by using the following series of commands:

Igor Stand: Igor stands slowly
Igor Walk: Igor stiffly walks
Igor Kill: Igor strangles the salesperson.

After killing each victim Igor goes back to his place and lies down.

The Skit ends with the mad scientist going to the front of the stage wringing his hands. *(He can no longer see Igor).* I can conquer the world, he says, with just three simple commands:

Igor Stand: Igor stands slowly
Igor Walk: Igor stiffly walks
Igor Kill: Igor strangles the mad scientist.

The Firing Squad

Participants: Minimum of 6.
Props: Toy rifles or sticks are optional.

A firing squad lines up as if to shoot a prisoner. Just as the time comes the prisoner yells, "Earthquake!", and the firing squad runs off, allowing the prisoner to escape. Another prisoner is brought forward, and this one escapes after yelling, "Tornado." This can be repeated with earthquake, avalanche, etc. The final Scout is brought out having seen the others and he attempts to do the same thing. Just as the firing squad is getting ready, this Scout yells "Fire", and the firing squad does.

Letters from Home

Participants: 2
Props: 2 sheets of paper.

It helps to have each Scout write their script on a piece of paper. They can read from the script, and pretend to be reading from the letters.

Scout 1: Hey, I got a letter from home!
Scout 2: So did I! What does your letter say?
Scout 1: Well, my brother says his doctor told him he needs to work out with dumbbells. He wants to know if I can exercise with him when I get home.
Scout 2: My Mom says she is writing this letter very slowly, because she knows I can't read fast.
Scout 1: My dad got a new job with 500 men working under him. He's cutting grass at the cemetery.
Scout 2: My dad lost his job delivering flowers. Apparently he was afraid to go into people's houses. His doctor says he was a classic example of a petrified florist.

Scout 1: Our neighbors started keeping pigs. My Dad got wind of it this morning.

Scout 1: My sister had a baby. She doesn't say if it's a boy or girl, so I'm not sure if I'm an Aunt or an Uncle.

Scout 2: Oh, there's a PS, it says I was going to send you $10.00, but I already sealed the envelope.

Scout 1: Throw me some paper so I can write back.

Scout 2: I can't toss it if it's stationary.

Green Side Up

Participants: 4 minimum.
Props: None.

SPL: Troop 7 has undertaken a project to restore this park.

The Scouts begin work on the project. The SPL remains at center stage. An adult approaches the SPL and begins an audible dialog with him(it doesn't matter what they discuss). The Senior Patrol Leader keeps interrupting their conversation to yell to the other Scouts, "Green Side Up." Finally the adult speaks.

Adult: What is it you keep yelling to them?
SPL: Oh, they're putting in sod and I just want to make sure they put the correct side up this time.

Peculiarity

Participants: 2.
Props: None.

Scout 1: Hello, Jim.
Scout 2: Helllllooo Bob.
Scout 1: Do you always stutter.
Scout 2: Nnnnoooo. Only when I I I tallk.
Scout 1: How come you stutter?
Scout 2: It's my p-p-peculiarity. Everyone has
              s-some p-p-peculiarity.
Scout 1: Oh yeah. I don't.
Scout 2: D-d-don't you stir your c-c-coff-eeee with your r-r-r-right
              hand?
Scout 1: Yes.
Scout 2: See that's your p-p-peculiarity. Most people use a spoon.

The Trained Elephant
(Dimbo the Elephant)

Participants: 3 plus volunteers.
Props: A poncho and a canteen.

An announcer and two additional Scouts perform in this skit. Two Scouts walk together with a poncho draped over them. The front Scout swings his arm back and forth like an elephant swings his trunk. The Scout in the back carries a canteen filled with water (The canteen is hidden under the poncho). The announcer states that he is an elephant trainer and he has trained his elephant, Dimbo, to carefully walk over people. The announcer asks for a brave volunteer to come forward so Dimbo can demonstrate his skill. A volunteer is selected, and the volunteer lays on the ground. Dimbo slowly steps over the volunteer. Two additional volunteers are chosen, and these volunteers lie alongside the first, spaced about two feet apart. Once again Dimbo gracefully steps over each of them. Finally, the trainer announces that he would like Dimbo to have a chance to break the world record by successfully walking over 5 Scouts. Are there two more volunteers? Dimbo begins to walk over the volunteers and the Scout who is playing the back end of Dimbo pours water on each of the volunteers that are laying underfoot. The announcer ends the skit by saying it looks like Dimbo had a little accident or you can just let the volunteers jump up and return to their seats.

The Viper

Participants: 3 minimum.
Props: None.

This skit can be done in a variety of settings. The basic idea is that a Scout comes in and proclaims that the viper is coming, the viper is coming. Everyone who hears the news becomes upset and begins repeating the statement, "The viper is coming." The skit ends when a Scout comes in with window washing equipment and says, "I'm the Vindow Viper. I've come to vipe your vindows."

The Rescuers

Participants: 3.
Props: None.

This skit requires three Scouts. One Scout is lying on the floor.
Two others come walking in.

Scout 1:   Look, this guy is badly hurt. *(Scout 1 checks his vital signs)* He's got no heart beat. We need to do CPR. *(Scout 2 joins Scout 1 on the ground and they begin CPR).*

Scout 2:   One, two, three, four, five, breathe......I'm getting tired, I think we'd better switch. *(At this point, Scout 3, the injured party ,gets up, Scout 2 lies down and they begin CPR on Scout 2).*

The Lost Neckerchief Slide

Participants: 2.
Props: None.

Scout 1:   *Searches around the campfire for a lost neckerchief slide.*
Can you help me? I've lost my neckerchief slide.

Scout 2:   Do you remember where you were standing when you lost it?

Scout 1:   Yes, over in that pine grove.

Scout 2:   Over there?
Scout 2 points into the darkness.

Scout 1:   Yea, that's the spot.

Scout 2:   Then why are you looking for the slide over here?

Scout 1:   Are you kidding? It's dark over there.

The Uniform

Participants: 2.
Props: Full dress uniform.

This skit requires two Scouts, an announcer and a demonstrator. The demonstrator Scout stands motionless at complete attention throughout the skit. The announcer uses the following monologue:

The Scout uniform is a source of great pride among Scouts. My assistant and I are here tonight to demonstrate the features of the uniform, as well as the proper way to wear it. I'd like to draw your attention to the neckerchief. See how a properly worn neckerchief compliments the uniform. *(Scout 1 move the neckerchief slide up and the demonstrator Scout pretends to be choking)*. Next make careful note of the rigid collar *(bend the collar up and leave it like that)*. These collars are specially made to stay in place.... *Continue to point out various features of the uniform with the goal of making the demonstrator look like a complete mess. Turn the pockets inside out(You can fill the pockets with cookie crumbs, candy or lint), roll up one of the sleeves, unbutton the shirt, remove a sock, etc. When the demonstrator is as disheveled as is possible, close the skit.* As you can see the Scout uniform is a source of great pride among Scouts. Wear your uniform with honor like my faithful assistant.

The Lawn Mower

Participants: 2 plus volunteers.
Props: None.

Scout 1 serves as the announcer, a second Scout acts like a lawn mower. Scout 1 pretends to pull the string in order to start the mower. The mower(Scout 2) sputters, but refuses to start. The first Scout then calls for volunteers to try and start the mower. The final volunteer successful starts the mower, and the announcer says, "I guess all it took to start the mower was a big jerk.

Reporter's First Scoop

Participants: 5.
Props: None.

A reporter is standing on the Brooklyn Bridge, about to jump. He is depressed because he can never get a big story ahead of the other writers in town. One by one others come along who have failed miserably in life. A teacher who hates kids, a boat captain who gets seasick, a gardener with hay fever, a construction worker afraid of heights, etc. Each is depressed and each decides to jump alongside the reporter. In the end they stand at the bridge and the reporter yells one, two, three. Everyone except the reporter jumps. The reporter takes out his notebook and yells, "What a scoop!" "Four people jump to gruesome deaths!"

Three Rivers

Participants: 2.
Props: A dog, plates, and silverware.

An elderly hermit is seated around the campfire making stew. A lost Scout comes upon the hermit, hungry from days in the woods without food. The Scout explains his predicament, and the hermit readily offers the Scout some food. The hermit grabs a dirty looking bowl for the Scout and is about to fill it with stew when the Scout says, "Gee, that plate seems kind of dirty." The hermit replies, "That plate ain't dirty, I tell you it's as clean as Three Rivers can get it. Yup, that plates as clean as Three Rivers can get it." The hungry Scout shrugs it off, and then eats the food that the hermit dishes out. When they are done eating the Scout says, "That food was mighty good, it really hit the spot." The hermit says, "Well, I guess its time to clean the dishes. Three Rivers, here boy, three rivers, here boy..." *A dog comes running over and begins to lick the plates.* "Good dog, Three Rivers, good dog."

Death Scene

Participants: 3 minimum.
Props: None.

A Scout who is a real over-actor plays the part of a soldier who has been fatally wounded and is about to die. He is not wearing dog tags so the medics cannot identify the soldier. Repeated they ask his name and the soldier responds by repeatedly crying phrases like help, water, medic, etc. Finally, the medic tells the soldier that he is about to die and they need to know his name so they can tell his mother. The soldier finally speaks his first sentence, "My mother already knows my name!"

Someone Chanted Evening

Participants: 4 minimum.
Props: None.

The scene is a monastery where a group of Monks has just risen for their morning prayers.

Friar:	Good morning everyone.
Monks:	Good morning friar.
Friar:	Let's warm up our voices this morning with a simple chant, Morning, morning mor-or-ninggg.
Monks:	(*not quite in unison*) Morning, morning mor-or-ninggg.
Friar:	Not bad, but we need to be a little more together. How about a little more energy and enthusiasm too. (*again not quite in unison*) Morning, morning mor-or-ninggg).

Finally on the third attempt everyone is in perfect unison except one monk clearly and loudly sings "Ev-e-ning"

Friar: Cut, cut, cut. That was all wrong.
One Monk: Why friar I thought that was good.
Friar: No, no, no. Clearly...*(breaking into song)* Someone Chanted Evening!

Leaky Submarine

Participants: 3 plus 1 volunteer.
Props: None.

This skit begins with 3 Scouts walking on stage. Each Scout is holding a cup, the lead Scout, who is acting as the commander, is holding two cups. The commander explains that his patrol is small and he needs a volunteer to help with this next skit. A volunteer is selected and placed in line between the other two Scouts from the patrol. The Commander explains that he is in charge of the submarine and each of his assistants work in the torpedo room. He hands an empty cup to the volunteer explaining that these paper cups are torpedoes. The group is organized in a line and the commander says, "Fire torpedo one". This phrase is passed down the line until the end Scout throws his cup into the fire. This routine is repeated again, this time with the volunteer throwing his paper cup into the fire. As they begin the third round the commander begins to say "Fire torpedo th...", when he stops in mid sentence and yells, "incoming torpedo, incoming torpedo." The second Scout on line says, "Captain, we've sprung a leak in torpedo chamber two," and throws his cup, which is filled with water, on the volunteer.

Incredible Odds

Participants: 3 minimum.
Props: None.

A small group of Scouts come out onto the stage (for this example we'll use 3) looking like they've just been in a terrible fight. They converse using language like, "What a fight, what a battle, we should never have taken those guys on in the first place, 3 against 100, in the face of incredible odds," etc. The performers should really build the situation up. Finally, the skit ends when one Scout says, "You know those were the toughest three guys I've ever seen."

Slow Motion Theft

Participants: 3.
Props: A comb, wallet, jackknife, keys, etc.

Two pickpockets announce to the crowd that they will demonstrate their incredible skill at their profession. A pedestrian comes walking toward them, and the pickpockets walk up to him, quickly brush up against him and continue to walk by. When the pedestrian disappears, they show all the things they stole from him (use whatever is handy like a wallet or jackknife, be sure to show a lot of stuff).

The pickpockets then ask the audience if they would like to see in slow motion, how the theft was done. They return the stuff to the pedestrian(Make sure the pedestrian puts the stuff in pockets where it will fall out easily) and re-enact the routine walking super slow. The pickpockets bump into the pedestrian, pick him up, turn him upside down and shake him vigorously until all the stuff falls out. The pickpockets drop him on the ground, pick up the stuff, put it in their pockets, pick up the pedestrian, set him back on his feet and all parties continue on their way.

Jail Thugs

Participants: 4 to 8.
Props: Deck of Cards.

Scouts act as if they are prisoners in "jail." A guard enters the area and yells "lights out!" The Scouts pretend to all go to sleep, and as soon as the guard leaves they get up and begin playing cards. One Scout asks all of the others what they did to get sent to jail. Each answers with a story like "I robbed a bank." Scouts respond favorably to each story up until you reach the last scout. The last Scout says, "You know those tags on mattresses that say 'Do Not Remove Under Penalty of Law'? Well I cut one off."

The other scouts all scatter screaming in fear and horror.

Peanuts

Participants: 5.
Props: None.

The lifeguard takes a group of Scouts over to the ranger.

Lifeguard: Here's a group of trouble makers ranger.
Ranger: Don't worry, I'll take care of them.
(lifeguard leaves)
Okay. Spit it out. What did you two do?
Scout 1: Nothing. I just threw peanuts into the lake.
Scout 2: It's true. All we did was throw peanuts into the lake.
Ranger: *(Turns to the third Scout)* Is this true? What do you have to say for yourself.
Scout 3: I'm Peanuts sir!

The World's Ugliest Man

Participants: 4 plus 1 volunteer.
Props: A Sheet.

The master of ceremonies brings out a Scout who is covered by a blanket. The MC explains that this is the world's ugliest man. This man is so ugly that no one can bear to look at his face without screaming and falling to the ground dead.

The master of ceremonies asks for volunteers to view the world's ugliest man. He selects a "plant" from audience and instructs the "plant" to stand face forward behind the world's ugliest man. The sheet is lifted so that only the volunteer can see the world's ugliest man. The volunteer screams and falls to the ground. This continues with several more "volunteer plants" coming forward viewing, screaming and fainting. Finally, the MC picks a Scout, or preferably, a Scoutmaster from another patrol or troop. When the sheet is raised the world's ugliest man screams and faints.

Sticky Gum

Participants: 4 minimum.
Props: None.

This is another one of those skits with lots of variations. Here's one way to perform the Sticky Gum Skit.

The skit begins with one Scout on stage chewing gum. He gets called away and before he goes he sticks the gum somewhere like on a tree. After he disappears, another Scout comes forward and leans against the tree into the gum. This Scout shakes the gum off his hand onto the ground. This Scout exits and another Scout come on stage and steps in the gum. This Scout scrapes the gum off his shoes onto a park bench and then leaves. Another Scout enters, sits on the bench and leans his hand into the gum. He gets up and scrapes his hand against the tree to get rid of the gum. He exits and the original Scout enters the stage. He says something like, "lets see, what was I doing. Oh yeah," and walks up to the tree, takes the gum, puts it in his mouth, starts chewing and walks offstage.

The Fisherman

Participants: 4 minimum.
Props: Sticks, string and worms.

A group of Scouts sit in a line holding sticks with string hanging from them. They pretend to cast, and all the Scouts but one, complain about how they are not catching anything. The one "quiet" Scout pretends to reel one fish in after another. Finally one of the Scouts asks the successful fisherman what his secret is. The fisherman mumbles an unintelligible response. No one understands what he said so they ask again, "What's you're secret to catching so many fish?" Finally, the successfully fisherman spits worms into his hands and replies, "You have to keep the worms warm."

Did You Sneeze?

Participants: 4 minimum.
Props: None.

A line of soldiers comes marching along. The last soldier in the line sneezes, and the commander, who is first in line, turns around and asks, "Did you sneeze?" The second soldier in line responds, "No," the leader calls him a liar, and whacks him on the side of the head. The soldier falls out of line and troop continues to march.

This process continues with each soldier being whacked out of the line until all that remains is the commander and the last soldier. The soldier sneezes and the commander asks, "Did you sneeze?" The soldier responds, "Yes, sir." The commander replies, "God Bless You" and they march away.

Good for Nothing

Participants: 2.
Props: None.

This skit requires a Scout, and a Scoutmaster who doesn't take himself too seriously.

Scout: *walking toward a Scoutleader* If I'm good throughout the entire camping trip will you give me $10.00?
Scoutleader: When I was your age, I was good for nothing.

The Pickpockets

Participants: 2.
Props: A comb, wallet and a pair of underwear.

Two old friends meet and embrace each other. They talk about what they've been up to, and both reveal that they've become pickpockets. The first exclaims that he is by far the best pickpocket in the world. The second responds that, he, in fact, is the better pickpocket. To prove it, he reveals the comb and wallet belonging to the first pickpocket, explaining that he stole them when they embraced. The first pickpocket replies, "That's nothing, look what I took from you." The first pickpocket reveals a pair of underwear; the second pickpocket peers into his shorts to see that his underwear are missing, grabs the underwear from the first, and runs off stage.

Latrine Miscommunication

Participants: 1 plus 3 volunteers.
Props: None.

Three volunteers are selected from the audience and are taken away from the stage where they can no longer hear the announcer. The volunteers are told that this is a contest. They are each instructed to act out an assigned part, and they are then told that the audience will be trying to guess who or what they are. The first volunteer is told to act like a jockey; the second is told to act like a fighter plane pilot, and the third is instructed to act like a bulldozer.

At the campfire, the MC has told the audience that these three Scout have been at camp all week and have been unable to use the bathroom. The audience thinks that they will be acting out their first trip to the latrine in a week. Needless to say, this miscommunication can have interesting results.

Football Superstar

Participants: 4 minimum.
Props: A doll.

The scene is a fire at a high rise building. One Scout plays the role of a father on the third floor of the burning building, another Scout serves as the football superstar, the rest of the patrol acts as the crowd. The father is yelling, my baby, my baby, somebody save my baby. The football superstar comes forward and claims that he is the greatest receiver to ever play the game. Just throw the baby down from the burning building and he will surely catch it. The father throws the baby and the crowd ou's and ah's as the baby is drifting far from the football superstar. At the last minute the superstar catches the baby on the dead run and the crowd cheers. Then the football superstar spikes the baby into the ground.

Crossing the Delaware

Participants: 4 minimum.
Props: Rowboat (optional).

If a rowboat from camp is available, it makes this skit work much more effectively. A group of Scouts are sitting in a rowboat. One of the Scouts stands in the front and plays the part of George Washington. The MC introduces this group as George Washington and his men crossing the Delaware. The MC gives this situation a big buildup, describing how tired the troops must be and suggests that everyone listen to George Washington's inspirational direction as they reach shore.

As he is finishing speaking the Scouts sitting in the boat begin to yell, "Hooray we've reached shore." George Washington waves his arms for silence and says, "Okay everybody, get out of the boat."

CPSIA information can be obtained
at www.ICGtesting.com
Printed in the USA
BVHW041115110819
555609BV00020B/689/P